Roaring Lions

A Majestic Coloring Book for Adults

This book belong to

____

____

Welcome to "Roaring Lions: A Majestic Coloring Book for Adults." In this book, you will discover a world of intricate designs and beautiful illustrations inspired by the king of the jungle: the lion. From the impressive manes of the male lions to the fierce determination of lionesses on the hunt, each page is a stunning tribute to these majestic creatures.

Whether you're a seasoned artist or simply looking for a way to unwind and relax, this coloring book offers a unique and engaging experience. With more than 80 illustrations to choose from, you'll be transported to the African savannah, where lions roam free and rule the land.

So grab your favorite coloring tools and let your creativity run wild as you bring these magnificent creatures to life. From bold and vibrant hues to subtle and nuanced shades, the possibilities are endless. "Roaring Lions: A Majestic Coloring Book for Adults" is the perfect way to unwind, de-stress, and discover your inner artist.

Lions: What you need to know

Lions are majestic creatures that belong to the Panthera genus, which also includes tigers, leopards, and jaguars. They are the second-largest living cat species after tigers and are native to Africa, as well as a small population in India. Lions are characterized by their impressive manes, which are unique to males and grow larger and darker as they mature.

Lions are social animals and typically live in prides, which consist of several females, their offspring, and a few males. Prides can have anywhere from 5 to 40 individuals and are led by a dominant male, known as a "lion king." Female lions are responsible for hunting for the pride and work together to take down large prey such as buffalo, zebra, and wildebeest.

Despite their formidable hunting abilities, lions do not exist in certain regions, including the Mid-East, North America, and Europe. This is because these regions have different environmental conditions that make it difficult for lions to thrive. In Africa, where lions are most commonly found, the terrain and climate are well-suited to their needs. However, in other parts of the world, the lack of suitable prey, competition from other predators, and changes in habitat have made it challenging for lions to survive.

Lions are apex predators and have few natural enemies in the wild. They are incredibly fast runners and can reach speeds of up to 50 miles per hour when chasing their prey. Their powerful legs and muscular bodies allow them to hunt effectively and cover long distances in pursuit of their next meal.

When it comes to reproduction, female lions typically give birth to a litter of 2-4 cubs after a gestation period of around 3.5 months. The cubs are born blind and rely on their mother for milk and protection. As they grow, the cubs learn how to hunt and survive in the wild, under the watchful eye of their mother and the rest of the pride.

Lions are highly adaptable creatures and have evolved over time to thrive in their environment. For example, their sandy-colored coats provide excellent camouflage in the African savannah, making it easier for them to sneak up on prey. Additionally, their sharp claws and powerful jaws allow them to catch and kill prey efficiently, while their strong social bonds and complex communication systems help them work together to achieve their goals.

Despite their impressive adaptations and natural abilities, lions face many threats today, including habitat loss, poaching, and conflict with humans. As a result, they are listed as a vulnerable species by the International Union for Conservation of Nature, and efforts are underway to protect and conserve these majestic animals for future generations.